Charles Smith

Report on the most powerful rifled guns, howitzers and mortars existing on October 1, 1880

Charles Smith

Report on the most powerful rifled guns, howitzers and mortars existing on October 1, 1880

ISBN/EAN: 9783337101435

Printed in Europe, USA, Canada, Australia, Japan

Cover: Foto ©Andreas Hilbeck / pixelio.de

More available books at **www.hansebooks.com**

REPORT

ON THE MOST POWERFUL

RIFLED GUNS, HOWITZERS, AND MORTARS

EXISTING ON OCTOBER 1, 1880,

BY

CAPT. CHAS. S. SMITH,

ORDNANCE DEPARTMENT, U. S. A.

WASHINGTON:
GOVERNMENT PRINTING OFFICE.
1880.

APPENDIX 26.

A SET OF TABLES AND PLATES, SHOWING PRINCIPAL DIMENSIONS AND ELEMENTS OF FIRE OF THE MOST POWERFUL RIFLED GUNS, EXISTING OR PROPOSED, AT THE COMMENCEMENT OF THE YEAR 1880; AND ALSO OF THE VARIOUS EUROPEAN RIFLED HOWITZERS AND MORTARS.

PREPARED BY CAPT. CHARLES S. SMITH, UNDER THE DIRECTION OF LIEUT. COL. S. CRISPIN, CONSTRUCTOR OF ORDNANCE.

(Fourteen plates.)

SIR: As requested by you, I have prepared, and herewith respectfully submit, a set of tables, with plates, giving the principal dimensions and elements of fire of the most powerful rifled guns, existing or proposed, at the commencement of the year 1880; and also of the various European rifled howitzers and mortars. Much of the information on rifled howitzers and mortars has already appeared in Ordnance Notes, No. 68; but it is here supplemented by the results of more recent experiments and the addition of some larger calibers, and altogether presented in a more summary shape.

The table of rifled guns has been prepared from the most reliable information available, and while it may not, in every particular, be absolutely correct, it will yet show closely enough what are the actual figures, to serve for the purpose of comparison.

To refer more particularly to this table, it will be seen that both the Italian and the English 100-ton Armstrong guns are included—the object being to show the respective powers of those two guns with regard to the particular powders employed. The Italian "progressive powder" has given excellent results, in admitting of the use of very large charges and the consequent attainment of high velocities, without subjecting the gun to any injurious pressures; at least, such was its record up to the bursting of the 100-ton gun on board the Duilio, a disaster which certain English writers have sought to attribute to the uncertain and dangerous action of the "progressive powder" rather than to a weak point in the gun itself. The Italian Government originally ordered from Armstrong's works eight of these 100-ton muzzle-loading guns for the turrets of the Duilio and Dandolo; afterwards eight more were ordered for the Italia and the Lepanto, which are to be *breech-loaders*, with the French system of fermeture.

The English 80-ton gun is the type of gun selected for the armament of the Inflexible. The four 100-ton guns purchased from Sir William Armstrong & Co. are intended for the works at Gibraltar and Malta, and were procured at a period when the exigencies of national affairs did not admit of the delay necessary for the fabrication and preliminary trial of the monster guns—160 to 200 tons—proposed by the Woolwich authorities. Since the disasters which have befallen the 38-ton gun on board the Thunderer, and the 100-ton gun on board the Duilio, the drift of opinion in England seems to be settling strongly in favor of breech-loaders; since, with such guns, the possibility of double loading could not exist, while the full exposure of the chamber after each fire would afford an opportunity for its frequent examination. It is quite possible, also, that some change of detail, if not of metal, will be made in their system of construction, since, by the creation of a chamber, the

3

thickness of the inner steel tube, upon which the longitudinal strain is mainly thrown, is considerably reduced, and, as would appear from the bursting of the Duilio's gun, thereby rendered too weak to support that strain.

In addition to the French guns given in the table, that government possesses breech-loading rifles of 13″.59 and 10″.63 caliber, and of 48 and 27 tons weight, respectively. There are also being constructed at Ruelle several 70-ton guns entirely of steel, of the model of 1874, the construction of which is, briefly, as follows:

The gun consists of a steel body lined with a short steel tube and banded with steel hoops, the breech-closure being the French screw. The tube is of Bessemer steel, hammered, and afterwards tempered in oil; the hoops and body of the gun are hammered puddled steel. The steel body is composed of two parts united under shrinkage, and further secured by means of a clasp. In the operation of shrinking, the forward end of the breech portion is inserted into the rear end of the chase portion, the latter being heated up for that purpose.*

The French ascribe the superiority of *all-steel* cannon to those of cast-iron hooped and tubed with steel chiefly to their greater power of penetration; though they claim their ability still to construct a cannon on the latter system (model of 1870) of equal power to the steel by increasing the caliber slightly. Thus, a cannon of the model of 1870 should have a caliber of 25 centimeters to equal a steel gun of 24 centimeters. The cost of the former would be about 23,000 francs, as against 100,000 francs for the latter; but the increase in weight, of gun and ammunition, would exceed that of the steel gun by about six tons, which is a matter of some importance on shipboard.

The Schultz wire gun has also been tested in France up to a caliber of 6″.25, and so satisfactory were the results that an 80-ton gun is now being fabricated upon that system. The wires, under the requisite degree of tension, are wrapped round a central steel tube, but are neither brazed nor welded. A steel casing is finally shrunk on over the wire-wound portion. This mode of construction is thought to give a very strong gun, as regards tangential strains, while the cost is comparatively low, owing to the inexpensiveness of the plant.

The Russian Government includes among its heavy guns the 14-inch Krupp's breech-loading rifle. A few years ago a 14-inch cast-iron rifle, hooped with steel, and having the French breech screw, was under construction at Perm; but no accounts have been received of its trial.

The Krupp works have already determined on the model of a 125-ton gun; and since the successful trial of the 72-ton gun at Meppen last year, their ability to fabricate such a gun seems to be placed beyond question. Large numbers of heavy rifled guns of calibers below 12 inch have been furnished by these works to many of the European powers, as well as to Turkey, Egypt, Japan, and some of the South American States; and the same is true, though to a more limited extent, of the Armstrong works. The 11-inch rifles furnished by the latter to the Chinese Government are for the gun-boat service; that government has also some 38-ton Armstrong guns in the same service.

The Brazilian Government has, in its naval service, some 35-ton guns, manufactured by Whitworth, of fluid-compressed steel, and rifled upon the hexagonal principle.

The proposed American 12-inch breech-loading rifle—given in the table—while it embraces the main features of the model now definitely

* "Manuel D'Artillerie," par H. Lee Barzic, Lieut. de Vaisseau.

adopted, varies from it somewhat in details. It is shorter, for instance, by a full caliber, in length of bore, and heavier by some four or five tons. The adopted model will probably admit of a charge of 300 pounds of powder and have a total weight of about 50 tons. It should give an energy of 23,991 foot-tons at the muzzle, which would be sufficient to penetrate 44 inches of iron, or 35 inches at a distance of 1,000 yards.

The table includes certain guns of minor caliber—5".87, 6", 8", and 9".45, respectively—but of relatively great power, owing to the large charges employed.

It will be observed that these guns have a large chamber for the reception of the charge, and a commensurate length of bore for its consumption. The number of cubic inches allowed per pound of powder indicates also that there is considerable windage, or air-space, about the cartridge in the chamber. As it is chiefly due to this allowance of air-space that the employment of large charges, without overstraining the gun, has been rendered practicable, it may be interesting to examine briefly the underlying physical causes on which the effect of air-spacing depends.

I. The tension of an elastic fluid, supposing the temperature to remain constant, varies directly as the density, and the density varies inversely as the volume or space occupied. The precise laws* according to which these variations take place in the bore of a gun may not be absolutely determined; but it is enough for our present purpose to know that the greater the density of the gunpowder gas the higher will be its tension; and the more contracted the space in which a given charge is burned, or the larger the charge burned in a given space, the greater will be the density of the resulting gas. Hence, powder burned in its own volume should yield its maximum effect; and that this is the case is fully sustained by experiment.

In the above statement lies the fundamental principle involved in air-spacing.

II. The velocity of inflammation, or the rate at which the ignition is spread from one grain of a charge of powder to another, depends—other things being equal, as size, shape, and density of grain, diameter of cartridge, &c.—on the greater or less confinement under which the charge is fired; that is, it depends on the degree of *tension* of the gas in the first instants of explosion. As the tension is higher, so will the inflamed gas be propelled the more forcibly through the interstices of the charge, and consequently the more rapid the spread of the ignition. That this is so will appear from the following results of actual experiment.†

Trains of service powder, containing about 0.11 pound of powder to the linear foot, were fired under different conditions as to confinement.

	Velocity of inflammation.
On a plane surface in the open air	7.87 feet.
In an uncovered trough	8.13 "
In a linen tube	11.38 "
In the same tube placed in a trough	17.48 "
In the trough covered up	27.88 "

These velocities are considered less than those obtained in fire-arms for the reason that, in the latter, the powder is not only confined at the sides but at one end, which was not the case in the covered trough,

---

* Analysis and experiment alike prove that the *pressure* increases more rapidly than the density.

† Benton's Ordnance and Gunnery, pages 51–52

where the gas could expand in both directions.[*] A velocity of more than 300 feet can be obtained by burning quick-match inclosed in a cloth tube.

Experiments have also proved that the velocity increases with the sizes of cross-section of the train : that it is greater with fine-grained powder than for coarse, except where the interstices are too much reduced, as in the case, for instance, of mealed powder.

III. The velocity of combustion, or the rate of burning of each grain from its surface to its center, other things being equal, depends on the pressure or *tension* of the surrounding gas. On this point Messrs. Noble and Abel, in their report on experiments with fired gunpowder (pages 121–122), state as follows:

"Piobert's views, moreover, that the pressure exerts but a trifling influence upon the rate of combustion, appears to us entirely untenable. With a particular sample of service pebble-powder, we found the time required for burning a single pebble in the open air to be about two seconds. The same sample was entirely consumed in the bore of a 10″ gun, and must, therefore, have been burned in less than .009 of a second."

The fact has also been clearly established by recent experiments made in France, in which mealed powder was driven into a steel tube closed at one end, and then burned under a smaller and smaller orifice for the escape of the gas. Care was taken in filling the tube to have the column of powder of a constant length and density. These experiments proved that an augmentation of pressure was always accompanied by an increase in the velocity of combustion, and that this result was apparent for the most feeble increments of pressure. [†]

When we consider that a grain of powder is a substance more or less heterogeneous and porous, it should seem to follow, as a necessary result, that under great pressure the highly inflamed gases would be forced into the softer parts and interstices of the grain itself, and the velocity of combustion thereby enormously increased. That the combustion of the grains does not proceed in parallel layers from the surface to the center is sufficiently evident from the appearance of half-burned grains which have been picked up after discharge.

Now, bearing in mind the above considerations, it will be readily seen that in the burning of a charge of powder where a certain air-space or windage about the cartridge is allowed, we obtain to a greater or less degree, depending upon the amount of that air-space, the conditions essential to a slow, deliberate gasification of the charge. The portion of bore allotted to the charge being larger than where no windage is allowed, the tension of the gas first formed will be lower, and inflammation and combustion will proceed more slowly. As a consequence of this slower evolution of the gas, the inertia of the projectile will be more gradually overcome and the strain upon the gun will be less. The *maximum* tension also of the gas, owing to the larger space afforded for its expansion, and its consequently lower maximum density, will be less, and both the velocity of the projectile and the pressure per square inch on the bore of the gun will be diminished. The operation is analogous indeed to that which obtains by the employment of the larger grained and denser powders.

---

[*] Benton's Ordnance and Gunnery, pages 51–52.

[†] Sarrau assumes that the velocity of combustion is proportional to a positive power of the pressure; but since it increases less rapidly than the pressure, the exponent of that power must be less than unity.

As an illustration of the effect of air-spacing in thus reducing the velocity and pressure, the following results, extracted from the published record of recent experiments with a 38-ton gun at Woolwich, are presented:

No. of round.	Air-space, feet.	Charge pebble powder, lbs.	Shell, and weight, lbs.	Velocity, feet.	Pressure, tons per square inch.
2...............		110	Palliser, 703	1,408	21.8
4...............	1	110	Palliser, 703	1,311	15.2
6...............	2	110	Palliser, 697½	1,223	14.7
8...............	4	110	Palliser, 705	1,013	12.6
10...............	6	110	Palliser, 705	836	8.9
12...............	8	110	Palliser, 701	754	7.4
13...............	10	110	Palliser, 698	582	6.1

Here the air-space consisted in leaving, successively, an interval between the cartridge and the projectile of 0, 1, 2, 4, &c., feet.

Now, the practical application of these facts lies obviously in adding to the charge, and in that way increasing the velocity, until the latter reaches to the highest attainable point for the length of bore or powder-burning capacity of the gun; since we can at the same time keep down the pressure within safe limits by the due allowance of air-space. The length of the cartridge, however, must not be overlooked, for if that is too great relatively to the diameter, there will be a likelihood of the occurrence of those extremely dangerous tensions known as "wave pressures." The shorter and fuller the charge also, the more favorable is its state for total consumption in the gun. With most of the existing cannon, owing to their very limited length of bore, it is not possible to realize more than partially the vast increase of power thus attainable by means of air-spacing. Hence the necessity for new constructions, involving as their prominent features great length of bore and a suitably proportioned powder-chamber. For an assumed length of bore, the largest charge that can be usefully employed is determined from the number of the "volumes of expansion"—as English artillerists term them—the bore can contain; that is, the number of times that the volume of the bore can contain the volume of the charge. The lowest limit of this ratio, or the point below which no increase of the charge will sensibly augment the velocity, is, of course, first ascertained from actual experiment. So likewise for a given charge the appropriate length of bore must be determined from a consideration of this same ratio.

To complete our view of the subject, let us trace briefly the probable mode of action of the explosive or propelling force in the ordinary and in the chambered gun. In the first case, the various phenomena of explosion of the charge occur in a relatively short period of time; the resulting tension of the gas is high, and the projectile is subjected to an impulse sudden and violent, but which is soon exhausted from the relatively small weight of charge employed and the greatly increased space soon left by the movement of the projectile for the expansion of the gas. Hence we obtain, perhaps, the maximum effect per pound of powder, but also a relatively high strain upon the gun. In the second case, we obtain, with the air-space and a much larger charge, at first a slower, and then a more uniform and prolonged pressure upon the projectile. Motion is acquired more gradually, and, owing to the large volume of the gas and the great length of the bore, the projectile is subjected to a longer-continued action of the propelling force. We thus obtain ultimately a much higher velocity, but from the comparatively low tension of the gas no greater pressure on the walls of the piece than in the case of the unchambered gun.

Captain Noble and Mr. Abel, in the report already alluded to, thus describe the operation of discharge in the ordinary case.

"The charge of powder is not instantly exploded, but is generally ignited at a single point: the pressure (commencing at zero) goes on increasing at an extremely rapid rate until the maximum increment is reached. It still goes on increasing, but at a rate becoming gradually slower, until the maximum tension is reached, when the increase of density of the gas, aided by the combustion of the powder, is just counter-balanced by the decrease of density due to the motion of the projectile. After the maximum of tension is reached, the pressure decreases, at first rapidly, subsequently slower and slower." *

The more gradual action, then, of the propelling force, which, in the ordinary case, occurs only at an advanced stage of the combustion of the charge, and after the projectile has begun to move from its place, takes place from the outset where a suitable air-space is allowed.

Captain Rodman determined, from some experiments made in 1859, in which he employed cast-iron shells of different interior capacities, filled with one-fourth the weight of powder they had previously been found to contain, that "where the volume of powder bears a constant ratio to the space in which it is burned the pressure will be sensibly uniform."†

This conclusion, however, which is only a reasonable inference from Mariotte's law, will hardly apply without some qualification to the altered conditions of discharge in the bore of a gun, where the powder-gases seldom reach their extreme tension, owing to the enlarged space afforded for their expansion by the displacement of the projectile. And as this displacement occurs the more readily, accordingly as the weight of the projectile‡ is less in proportion to the area subjected to the action of the propelling force, we should expect, other things being equal, a higher tension of the gases, and therefore a greater pressure on the walls of the bore, as the caliber of the piece is enlarged. Hence the employment of coarser grained and denser powders, or, which is to the same effect, more allowance of air-space in the larger calibers.§

The control which, as we have seen, we thus obtain over the burning of gunpowder by means of air-spacing, opens a new field for investigation and progress in artillery. Already there is a tendency abroad to desist from the production of monster guns, and to employ instead guns of smaller caliber, but chambered for very large charges. Of course the latter feature necessitates a considerable increase in the length of

* If these variations in pressure be represented by a curve, it would commence at the origin convex to the axis of x, would then become concave, then again convex, and would finally be asymptotic to the axis of x.
In the same way the curve, representing the velocity, would commence by being convex to the axis of abscissæ; it would then become concave, and, were the bore long enough, would be finally asymptotic to a line parallel to the axis of x.— (Researches on Explosives: Fired Gunpowder. By Captain Noble and Professor Abel.)

† The same relation is expressed by the formula of Count Rumford, also deduced from the observed pressures in a close vessel.

‡ For similar projectiles, the area subjected to pressure increases as the square, while the weight—the resistance to be overcome—increases as the cube of the caliber.

§ So, too, for an increase of *charge* with the same caliber, the same proportional displacement of the projectile not occurring at so early an epoch there results an increase of tension.

he bore; a length of from 25 to 30 calibers not being deemed excessive where the weight of the charge equals one-half that of the shot. The great length thus entailed on the gun may, in some respects, prove a source of inconvenience. Another objection, suggested in connection with the high velocities attained and the comparatively light weight of the gun itself, is the severity of the recoil. This objection, however, is not insurmountable.

It has long been known that, by reducing the diameter of the cartridge, the strain on the gun might be diminished; but it does not appear that this knowledge was ever utilized for increasing the charge, and thus for adding to the velocity. As early as 1833 Captain Piobert, of the French artillery, proposed increasing the space in rear of the ball by diminishing the diameter of the cartridge, or by interposing an elastic wad between the powder and ball, in order to prevent the very rapid destruction of brass siege-guns, which is caused by the use of large charges.

Captain Mordecai, in his report of "Experiments on gunpowder," 1842-'45, states in his conclusions: "For the purpose of diminishing the strain on the gun, I propose that the principle of increasing the length of the cartridge, by reducing the diameter, should be adopted for heavy guns."

In referring also to the results of experiments made by a board of French officers at Metz, in 1836-'37, on reducing the diameter of the cartridge, he states: "Although the range of my experiments did not allow me to verify these results, I have permitted myself to make the foregoing remarks on the French experiments in order to call the attention of the Ordnance Department to a matter which may be of the greatest importance to us, in reference to giving increased durability to our iron guns, and diminishing the risk of accidents which have been lately of frequent occurrence from the bursting of these guns."

Captain Rodman also, in 1857-'58, made a series of experiments to determine "the effect of windage in the cartridge upon the pressure exerted by equal charges." His results confirmed those obtained by earlier experimenters.

It was not, however, until a very recent day that experiments is this direction took such shape as to result, finally, in the true application of this important principle, namely, in increasing largely the powder-charge.

During the experiments with the 80-ton gun in England in 1876-'77, when every effort was being made to increase the power without compromising the safety of that piece, the attention of the English authorities was directed to certain experiments being made in Germany with an increased air-space over the cartridge, by means of which larger charges were employed, with the attainment of higher velocities, and yet with moderate pressures.

Shortly after, the Armstrong 6-inch, and 8-inch, and the Krupp 5-inch and 9.45-inch chambered guns were produced, burning the enormous charges of one-half the weight of their projectiles, and with the attainment of the astonishing velocity of 2,100 feet—astonishing from the fact of the very moderate pressure accompanying it.

In connection with this subject of air-spacing, attention is called to a conclusion drawn from experiment by both Captains Mordecai and Rodman, which does not harmonize, wholly, with the foregoing deductions.

Captain Mordecai states that it appears from the results of his experiments, made with cartridges of different diameters and lengths, "That whilst the usual diameter of the cartridge for the 24-pounder gun as now established (5″.35) is favorable to the development of the force of the charge, no great diminution of effect arises from reducing the diameter to 5 inches; on the other hand, *the force of the charge is vastly reduced by increasing the diameter of the cartridge to the full size of the bore.*"

He then proceeds to account for the latter result (pp. 288–289, "Experiments on Gunpowder"). Captain Rodman states (p. 179, "Experiments on Metals for Cannon") in regard to the results obtained in his experiments on the effect of windage in the cartridge, in a 42-pounder S. B. gun, "These results, both pressures and recoils, indicate that *the pressure increases with the windage up to about one inch windage,* beyond which the pressures and recoils both gradually diminish as the windage in the cartridge increases."

This apparent anomaly will admit, perhaps, of explanation by reference to those principles we have had under consideration. To quote Captain Rodman's own words—used in another connection—"from the fact that there was no vacant space around the cartridge, all the powder that was burned before the shot moved must have been burned in its own volume, and the maximum pressure would be reached before the charge would be nearly consumed;" the force of the gas would thus be sufficient to roll forward the spherical shot, offering, as it does, but little resistance to motion, at an earlier epoch of the combustion than is usual, and the equivalent to an air-space be produced of greater extent probably than results with the employment of the service cartridge; hence a falling off in velocity and pressure.

It was not believed that such results would obtain in the case of a rifle-projectile, which offers a much greater resistance to motion; the following series of experiments, therefore, were undertaken at the Proving Ground, Sandy Hook, N. J., for the purpose of determining this point.

(1.) The gun employed was an 8-inch rifle, vented in the prolongation of the axis of the bore.

The record of firing was as follows:

| No. of rounds. | Charge. | | Weight of shot. | Windage over cartridge. | Mean. | |
	Kind of powder.	Weight.			Velocity.	Pressure.
		Pounds.	Pounds.		Feet.	Pounds.
1..........	Hexagonal, E. V. J.; density 1.75; grain, 72.	*35	180	Service windage about $\frac{1}{5}$ of the diameter of the bore.	1,382	30,500
2..........		30	180	Service windage.............	1,258	20,000
2..........		30	180	Service windage reduced 50 per cent.	1,263	23,000
2..........		30	180	None.....................	1,344	25,500

*Service battering charge.

Gain, due to entire suppression of windage, in { Velocity, 86 feet.
{ Pressure, 5,500 pounds.

ΓILE.

Means of rota-
tion

Bronze
and e:
ing gas-

Bronze :

Bronze :

Copper l

xpandir
    checl

xpandir
    checl

..do ...

..do ...

Of chamber.	No. groo
Inches.	
....	1
7. 0	2 (para
....	3 (cunei
....	.....
....	2
6. 06	1

/ITZERS AND

	Ra:
g	Weight of charg to weight o projectile.
:...|	1 to 12

r

V.—COMPARATIVE TABLE OF FIRE OF EUROPEAN 9-INCH RIFLED HOWITZERS AND MORTARS.

VI.—TABLE OF PRINCIPAL DIMENSIONS OF EUROPEAN 10 AND 11-INCH RIFLED HOWITZERS AND MORTARS.

VII.—COMPARATIVE TABLE OF FIRE OF EUROPEAN 10 AND 11-INCH RIFLED HOWITZERS AND MORTARS.

(2.) Gun employed, 3-inch breech-loading rifle, vented on top.
The record of firing was as follows:

No. of rounds.	Kind of powder.	Weight of charge.		Weight of shot.	Windage over cartridge.	Mean.	
		Pounds.	Ounces.			Velocity.	Pressure.
				Pounds.		*Feet.*	*Pounds.*
2	J. K.; grain, 2,200; density 1,725.	2	....	12¼	¹⁄₂₀ of the diameter of the bore.	1,269	20,250
2		2	....	12¼	None	1,318	24,750

Gain, due to entire suppression of windage, in $\begin{cases} \text{Velocity, 49 feet.} \\ \text{Pressure, 4,500 pounds.} \end{cases}$

These results, taken in connection with the others that have been given, would seem to establish, conclusively, the fact of the uniformity of operation of the laws involved in air-spacing; while at the same time they serve to explain the apparent exception.

VIII.—Table showing comparative practice with rifled howitzers and S. B. mortars.

Nature of piece.	Weight in cwts.	Caliber in inches.	Length—Of piece in inches.	Length—Of bore in inches.	Charge in pounds.	Weight of projectiles. (Pounds)	Bursting charge. (Pounds)	Elevation.	Range, yards.	Deviation in yards. Lateral.	Deviation in yards. In range.	Remarks.
English.												This table does not give the results with the service 8-inch R. M. L howitzer, but only the experimental practice, through the results of which we can compare S. B. mortars and rifled howitzers generally when firing about same charges.
13-inch mortar	100	13	53	39	10	204	11	0	2,930	55	63	
9-inch howitzer	76.2	9	76	54	10	200	7	15	4,742	10	23	
10-inch mortar	52	10	46	35	4.75	95	5.25	45	4,720	100	78	
8-inch howitzer	64	8	65.9	48	6	120	5.75	39	4,514	20	57	
American.												Fire of Prussian 21 c. m. B. L. rifled mortar.
13-inch S. B. mortar	152.85	13	56.5	35.1	*10 / 20	216	7	45	3,187 / 4,636			
10-inch S. B. mortar	65.17	10	49.25	32.5	7.5 / 12	101.67	2	45	3,471 / 4,536			

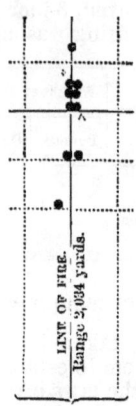

LINE OF FIRE.
Range 2,034 yards.

* Initial velocity, 761 feet.

HEAVY RIFLED GUNS.
ENGLAND.

8 INCH.   (Armstrong)
(11 Tons)

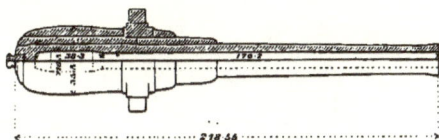

12·5 INCH.
(38 Tons)

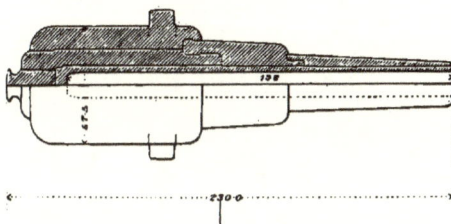

16 INCH.
(80 Tons)

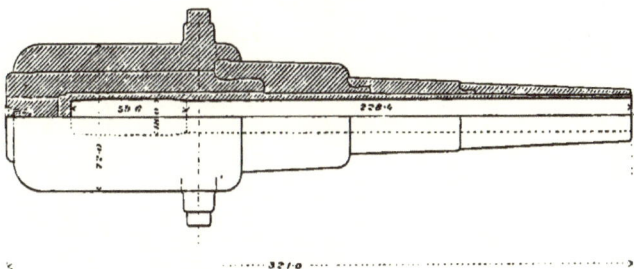

Scale

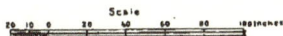

Appendix 26—1880.

PLATE II.

HEAVY RIFLED GUNS.
KRUPP'S WORKS.

9·45 INCH.
(18 Tons)

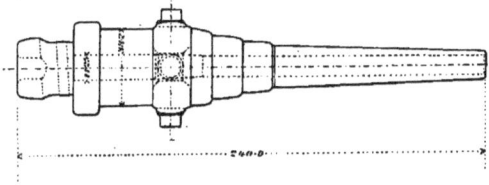

13·97 INCH.
(51 Tons)

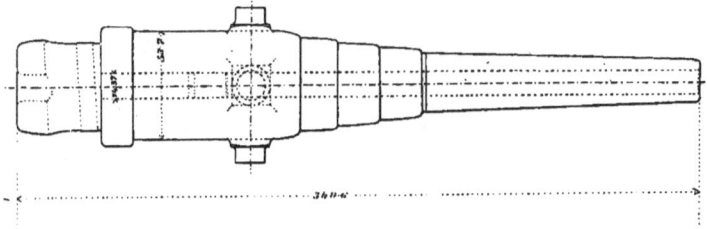

15·75 INCH.
(72 Tons)

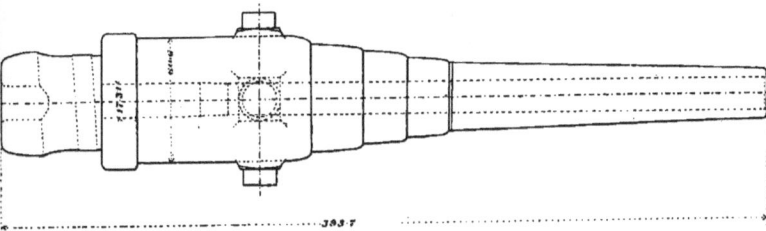

Scale.

Appendix 26—1880.

HEAVY RIFLED GUNS.
ITALY,

12·6 INCH.
(38 Tons)

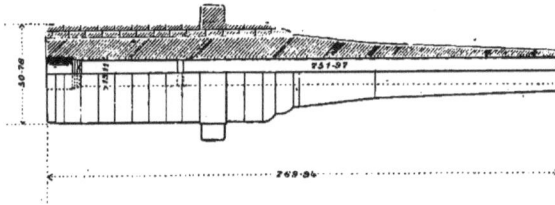

18·1 INCH.
(87 Tons)

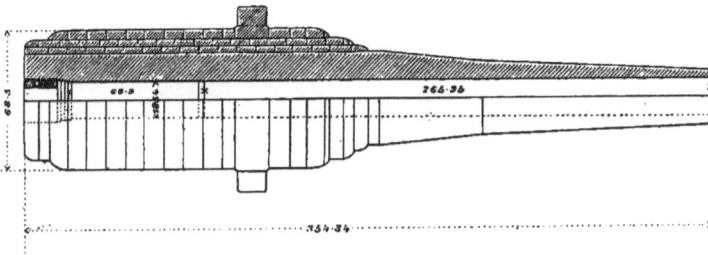

·17·7 INCH.   (Armstrong)
(100 Tons)

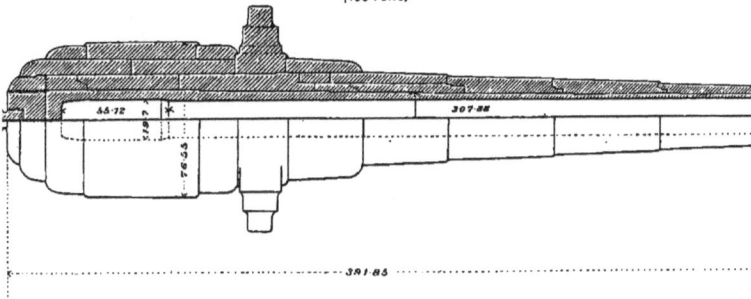

Scale.

Appendix 26—1880.

PLATE IV.

HEAVY RIFLED GUNS.

FRENCH 12·6 INCH.
(34 Tons)

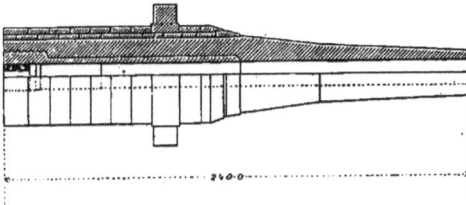

RUSSIAN 12 INCH.
(39 Tons)

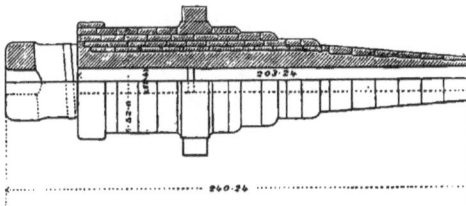

AMERICAN 12·25 INCH.
(44 Tons.)

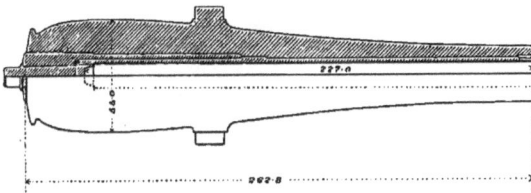

Scale.

Appendix 26—1880.

HEAVY RIFLED GUNS.

KRUPP 12 INCH.
(Probable Construction)
(36 Tons)

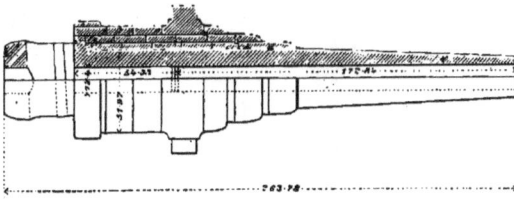

ENGLISH 12 INCH.
(Proposed Model)
(42 Tons)

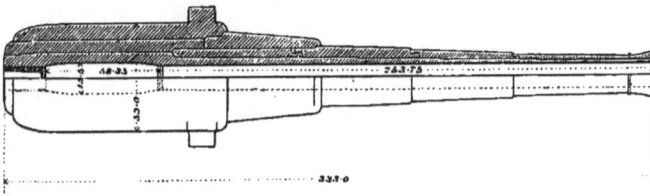

AMERICAN 12 INCH.
(Proposed Model.)
(55 Tons.)

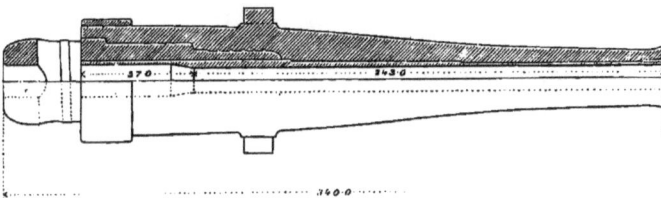

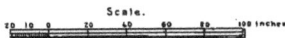

Scale.

Appendix 26—1880.

PROJECTILES

FOR

HEAVY RIFLED GUNS.

(CORED SHOT)

KRUPP.

Old Model.

New Model.

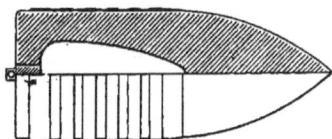
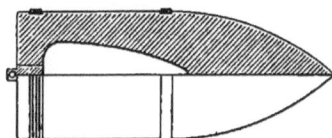

FRENCH.

ITALIAN.

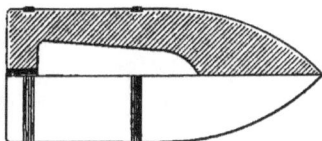
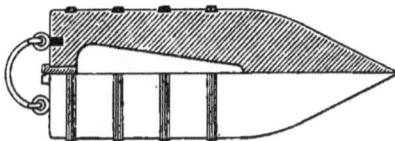

ENGLISH.

Old Model.

New Models.

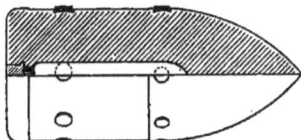
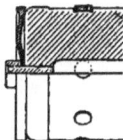

AMERICAN.

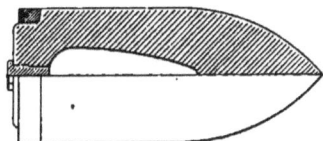
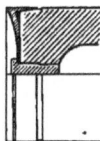
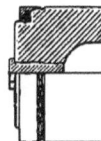

Appendix 26—1880.

PLATE VII.

RIFLED HOWITZERS AND MORTARS.
GERMANY.

8 INCH.

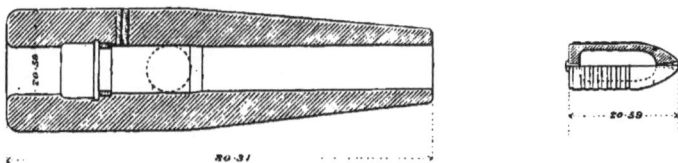

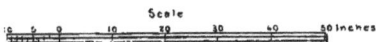

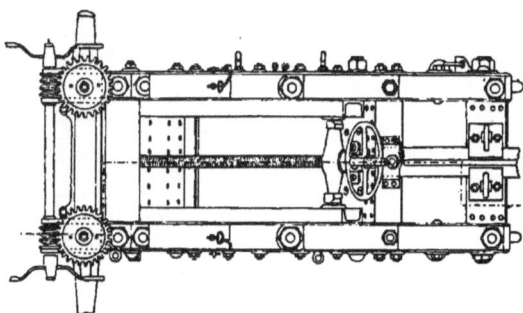

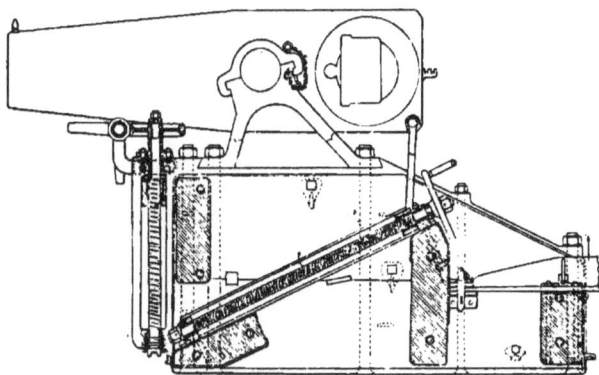

Appendix 26—1880.

PLATE VIII.

RIFLED HOWITZERS AND MORTARS.
KRUPP'S WORKS.

5·9 INCH.

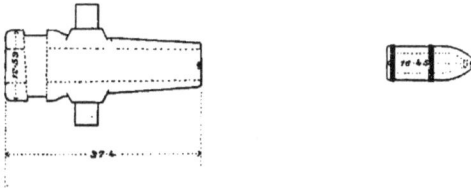

8·26 INCH.

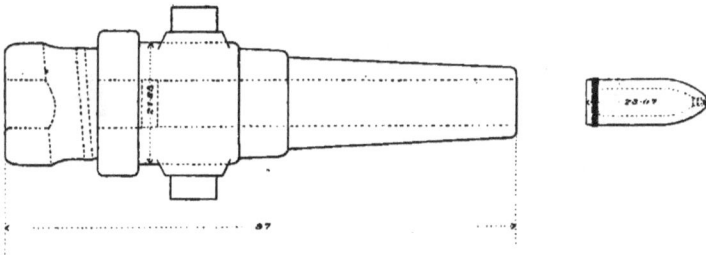

II INCH.

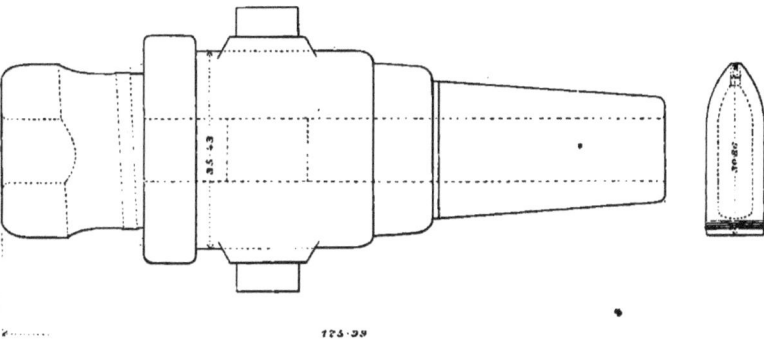

Scale.

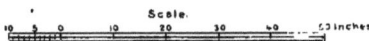

Appendix 26—1880.

PLATE IX.

RIFLED HOWITZERS AND MORTARS.

KRUPP'S WORKS.

8·26 INCH.

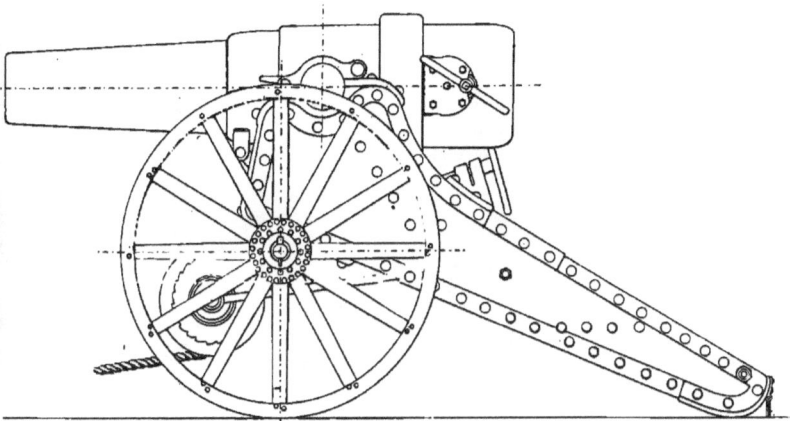

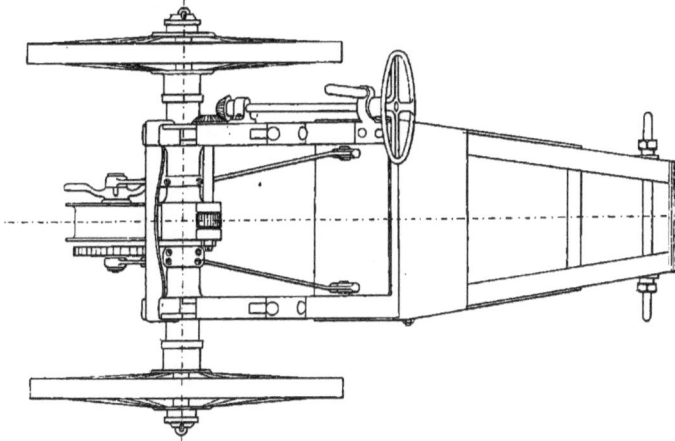

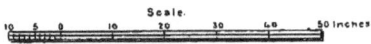

Scale.

10 5 0   10   20   30   40   50 Inches.

Appendix 26—1880.

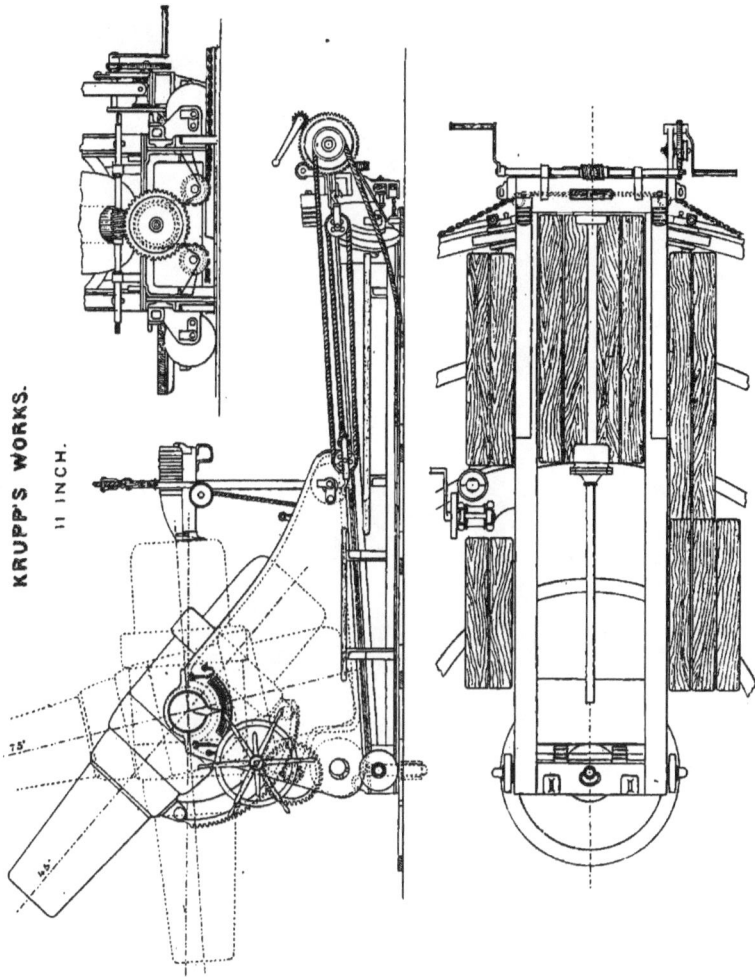

15°

45°

PLATE XI.

RIFLED HOWITZERS AND MORTARS.
RUSSIA.

6 INCH.

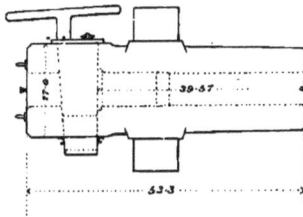

8 INCH.

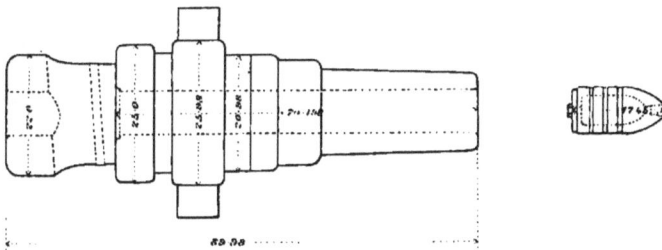

11 INCH.

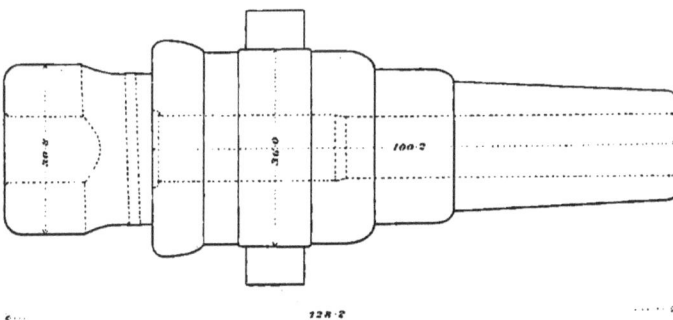

Scale.

Appendix 26—1880.

PLATE XII.

RIFLED HOWITZERS AND MORTARS.

5·9 INCH. KRUPP.

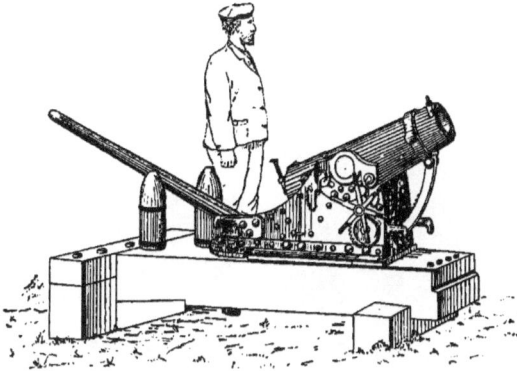

6 INCH. RUSSIAN.

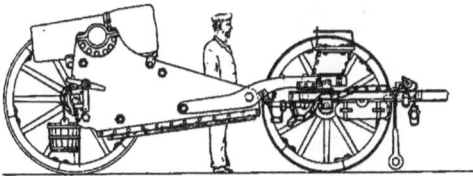

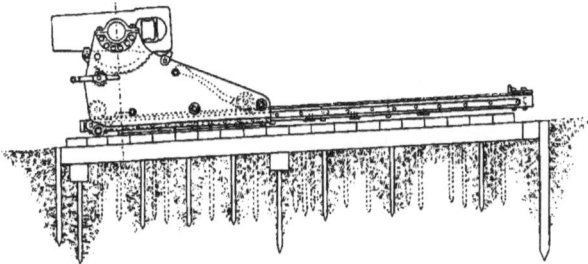

PLATE XIII.

RIFLED HOWITZERS AND MORTARS.

AUSTRIAN 8 INCH.

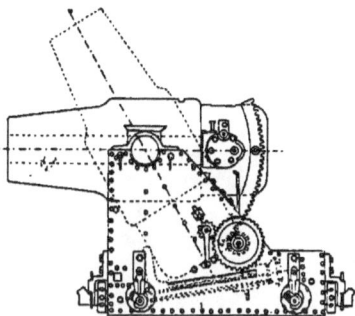

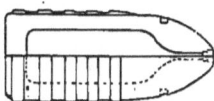

FRENCH 8·6 INCH.

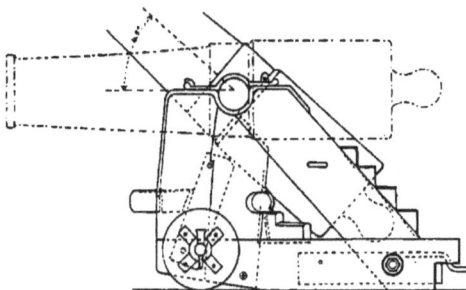

PLATE XIV.

RIFLED HOWITZERS AND MORTARS.
ENGLAND.

6·3 INCH.

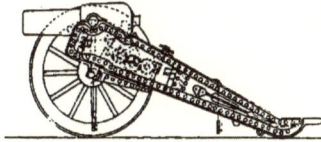

6·3 INCH.

8 INCH.

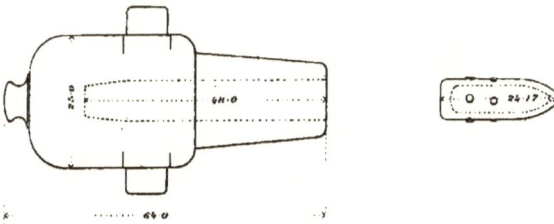

10 INCH.

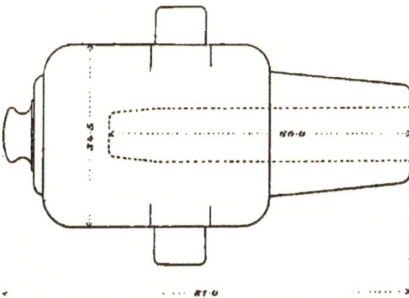

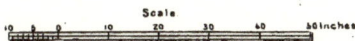

Scale

Appendix 26—1880.

www.ingramcontent.com/pod-product-compliance
Lightning Source LLC
Chambersburg PA
CBHW021552270326
41931CB00009B/1181